BBILE SUNDAY SCHOOL HANDBOOK FOR ADULTS

(2)

A non-denominational weekly topical
Bible study

ISBN: 9798371015303

Imprint: Independently published

TABLE OF CONTENTS

Preface

This book contains twenty six lesson carved out from some crucial areas of problems in Christianity. The purpose of these lessons is to rebuke, teach and correct brethren standing under Biblical platform. You will find these lessons interesting as you flip through the pages of this book. It is highly recommended for every Christian adults and ideal for use in churches, weekly fellowships and group bible study meetings. It is non-denominational

Bible Sunday School Handbook

for Adults (2)

CHAPTER ONE: FASTING

LESSON 1: WHEN AND WHY CHRISTIANS SHOULD FAST

TEXT: *Matthew 6:16 moreover when ye fast, be not, as the hypocrites, of a sad countenance: for they disfigure their faces, that they may appear unto men to fast. Verily i say unto you, they have their reward.*

MEMORY VERSE: *Matthew 26:42 He went away again the second time, and prayed, saying, O my Father, if this cup may not pass away from me, except I drink it, thy will be done.*

INTRODUCTION:

Fasting is a common practice even among non-Christians. It is frequently regarded as a way to access supernatural grace as well as a solution to a variety of bodily and spiritual issues. However, there are many hidden truths that need to be revealed in order for individuals to no longer be in the dark regarding when and why to fast. This lesson is aimed at providing biblical justification for when and why we fast as Christians.

WHEN AND WHY CHRISTIANS SHOULD FAST

1. **WHEN YOU ARE LED BY THE SPIRIT:** (MATTHEW 4:1) This is one of the most important information about when and why to fast; however, it is unfortunate the majority of Christians do not pay attention to this; perhaps due to the misconception that fasting is a method or part of prayer. Prayer and fasting are two completely different spiritual disciplines. Therefore, just because one has to pray does not necessarily mean that one must fast. When talking about when and why Christians should fast, Priority should be given to the Holy Spirit's leading and this can happen at any time because the Spirit may not act according to our schedule. In simpler words, this means that a Christian has

no specific time or reason for fasting until revealed by the Holy Spirit.

2. **WHEN SEEKING DIVINE DIRECTION** (DEUTERONOMY 9: 9-10, DANIEL 2:16-19, 10:3, ACTS 10 :30) A very good time to fast is as we have seen in these two scriptures when you are in need of divine direction, response or revelation from God.

3. **BEFORE EMBARKING ON MINISTRY OR ANY DIVINE ASSIGNMENT** (MATTHEW 4:1-2): Before starting his early ministry, Jesus fasted. He laid this as a foundation for us, demonstrating to us the value of fasting as a means of preparing for divine assignments. This refers to all types of divine instructions. To carry them out successfully, one must be spiritually and physically prepared and fasting is recommended in this case.

4. **WHEN INTERCEEDING SEEKING GOD'S INTERVENTION**: The Bible is rich with instances of individuals who fasted when an

immediate divine intervention was required. Queen Esther when in need of God's help to stand before the King, she instructed her maids and all the Jews in Shushan to fast (Esther 4:13-16). The old prophetess in Luke 2:36–37 fasted constantly as she intercedes for the coming of the Messiah. See further examples: (I King 19: 4- 8, Ezra 10:16-17, Nehemiah 1:14; 2:10). Fasting is advised whenever intercession or divine intervention is urgently needed.

5. **REPENTANCE** (JONAH 3:5): To show remorse and genuine repentance after hearing the message of Jonah, the Nenevites including their animals fasted. Fasting is a discipline that shows submission. Apart from the Nenevites, the Israelites also fasted a number of times in the Bible to indicate their return to God after whiling away in sin. David and some others in the Bible are individuals who exercise this discipline. Though sin should not be a deliberate act, when

it comes, to overcome it and be in right standing with God you need fasting

SUMMARY: From this lesson it is now clear that fasting can be anytime when the spirit leads, when seeking divine direction, when embarking on ministry or any divine assignment, when intercession and God's intervention is necessary and when in repentance you seek God's mercy.

QUESTION

1. Is it right to fast everyday of the week? if yes explain why

2. Mention when and why we should fast

LESSON 2: CONSIDERATIONS BEFORE FASTING

TEXT: *Matthew 6:16-18 Moreover when ye fast, be not, as the hypocrites, of a sad countenance: for they disfigure* *their faces, that they may appear unto men to fast. Verily I say unto you, They have their reward. But thou, when thou fastest, anoint thine head, and wash thy face; That thou appear not unto men to fast, but unto thy Father which is in secret: and thy Father, which seeth in secret, shall reward thee openly.*

MEMORY VERSE: Mark 11: 25 *And when ye stand praying, forgive, if ye have ought against any: that your Father also which is in heaven may forgive you your trespasses.*

INTRODUCTION

For a Christian, fasting is beneficial and crucial, but it can also go horribly wrong or be ineffective if certain factors are not taken into consideration. This lesson aims to make Christians who fast aware of the necessary preparations that must be made in advance to avoid problems with the discipline. This lesson explains why many Christians attempt fasting without seeing any benefit.

SOME FACTORS TO CONSIDER BEFORE FASTING

1. **SPIRITUAL STATE OR CONDITION**: (Mark 11:25, Matthew 6:14-15) your spiritual condition is something you should consider before beginning a fast. Because fasting is a spiritual practice, its main objective is to submit you before God. Therefore, you should be aware that it can only be perfected if you let go of past wrongs, offenses, and unpleasant feelings against other people. By doing this you are simply ready spiritually to fast.

2. **PHYSICAL/HEALTH STATUS**: (I CORINTHIANS 3: 16-17). Before embarking on a fast, take into consideration your general physical well-being or health. There are many activities that are out of the question due to our health, just as there are many activities that are off limits at specific ages, especially as we get older because the body requires certain

nutrients on a regular basis to maintain health at these times. The body is the Holy Spirit's temple (I Corinthians 6:19-20). The body should be taken care of and its health should not be despised.

3. **CONSIDER YOUR TIME AND WORKING SHELDUES**: (1 THESSONALONIANS 4:11-12, 2 THESSALONIANS 3:10-12). Before undertaking a fast, one must seriously consider this important issue. The **B**ible admonishes everyone to work for a living (Proverbs 14:23, 1 Timothy 5:8). Fasting shouldn't be used as an excuse for being idle or lazy. Therefore, before beginning a fast, think about the work you do, your work schedules, and the task you have at hand. Let them not struggle with your fasting. Before beginning a fast, take into consideration any difficult tasks which you must accomplish in order to avoid failing at working place, offending customers or clients, and most importantly dishonoring your

boss. It is improper to faint out or to fall sick while fasting. By taking this into mind, you can decide to fast during your free time, when you have a helper as regards your work, or better still limit the duration of hours in which you fast according to your strength.

4. **TRAVELING**: With some exceptions, this is also an important factor to consider. Traveling shouldn't have been an issue for anyone who is fasting unless for people who experience motion sickness when travelling. In this case it is necessary to consider the distance or circumstances surrounding the journey. Obviously, if you are traveling a longer distance it is inevitable that you will miss your scheduled prayer time or that your body system would become upset.

SUMMARY

Though fasting is of spiritual importance. These earlier mentioned out to be given attention order wise the fasting may be laborious, problematic, inflective NOTE it is called fasting and prayer therefore skipping meals alone does not make a fasting it must go with praying at intervals throughout the day. And these considerations will necessitate.

QUESTIONS

1. Mention the factors necessary for considerations before embarking on fasting
2. Can one go ahead and fast when all these factors are not favorable?

LESSON 3: BENEFITS OR IMPORTANCE OF FASTING

TEXT: Isaiah 58:6 *Is not this the fast that I have chosen? to loose the bands of wickedness, to undo* *the heavy burdens, and to let the oppressed go free, and that ye break every yoke?*

MEMORY VERSE 2 Chronicles 7:14 *If my people, which are called by my name, shall humble themselves, and pray, and seek my face, and turn from their wicked ways; then will I hear from heaven, and will forgive their sin, and will heal their land.*

INTRODUCTION:

One good reason why other religions like Judaism and Islam maintain the discipline of fasting as the Christians is because of its benefits. This lesson studies the benefits of fasting particularly to Christians.

1. **IT BENEFITS OUR HEALTH**: Fasting has shown to have a positive effect on our health. Staying without food for a period of time is health wise. In a lay man's explanation, it permits our digestive system to finish up the

digestion of the previous food eaten, rest and get re-energize for the next food to be eaten. This alone solve the problem of stomach ache, indigestion, constipation etc. fasting empowers our immune system in many ways and help us to keep fit. Please meet medical practitioners to learn more about this.

2. **IT HUMBLES US BEFORES GOD AND MEN**: It is a spiritual discipline. There is no better way of learning to follow Jesus and carrying our cross other than laying down ourselves. As Jesus mentioned in (Luke 9:23) when fasting a believer is completely reduced as a disciple full of discipline.

3. **FASTING HELPS US TO DEPEND ON GOD:** In fasting we are out of ourselves forgetting and overlooking the fact that we cannot do without food (Psalm 63: 1, Matthew 6: 33). In fasting we are seeking the kingdom in order that every other thing will be added to us.

4. **IT BOOSTS OUR SPIRITUAL SENEITIVITY**: This is very true about fasting and why this so is a mystery. In fasting nothing distracts us from hearing, seeing, interpreting spiritual revelation around us (Galatians 5: 16) this is what it means by working in the spirit

5. **IT LIMITES US FROM CARNALITY**: During fasting almost all believers are conscious of the things of the spirit thereby limiting the activities of the flesh. By this I mean one way in which fasting benefits us is we can easily stay away from sins while fasting and this helps our growth in faith. A chain smoker or drunker for instance when fasting knows what he is doing that he can't consciously indulge in the acts unless after the fast.

SUMMARY

Fasting is very important to our physical and spiritual it is highly recommended to go into it for the sake of the benefit listed above.

QUESTION

1. How important is fasting to our body?
2. How important is fasting to our spirit?

LESSON 4: WHEN FASTING IS NOT NECESSARY

TEXT: Hebrew 11: 6 *But without faith it is impossible to please him: for he that cometh to God must believe that he is, and that he is a rewarder of them that diligently seek him.*

MEMORY VERSE: Psalms 127: 2 *It is vain for you to rise up early, to sit up late, to eat the bread of sorrows: for so he giveth his beloved sleep.*

INTRODUCTION

There are times in our lives when we do things that are good and important but not required at the moment. Fasting is a very important spiritual discipline that every Christian should be encouraged to embark on but the truth is there are times when fasting are not required. This is what this lesson is all about.

1. WHEN IN DOUBT: Anything spiritual can never flourish in an atmosphere of doubt. Once doubt is introduced, neither fasting nor prayers are required not because they are not important but because they unnecessary. Jesus says that you can only receive when you believe in (Mark 11:24). Regardless of motivation, if there is no faith, fasting is useless and not necessary.

2. WHEN IT IS PLANNED AND NOT LED BY THE HOLY SPIRIT: Fasting must be as the spirit leads otherwise it is unnecessary (Matthew 4: 1). Some believers bring in fasting into their monthly schedules thinking it is spirituality but this is simply unnecessary for prayer alone

without fasting is still powerful. But for whatever reason fasting must be spirit led.

3. WHEN PHYSICALY CHALLENGED: Except for a spectacular reason fasting is not necessary for physically challenged. Especially those under medication, pregnant, breastfeeding mothers aged people, etc.

4. WHEN PRAYER IS NOT INVOLVED: This needs to be given a lot more attention, particularly in this part of the world where fasting is perceived to be limited to simple deprivation of food or water. Most believers don't give it much thought; they get up in the morning and stay until evening or after a set period of time, then claim to have fasted. However, it is unnecessary to fast if you only stay without food or water and didn't pray until few minutes when you are about to break the fast. The act of fasting combines abstinence from

food or drink with continuous prayer till the time is up.

5. **WHEN IT IS UNCONIOUSLY OBSERVED:** Some people have the ability to say without food and water for a long period of time whether or not they are fasting this could be as a result busy schedules, low appetite for food, or simply because they are broke. People like this shouldn't claim to be fasting when they actually are not. However, the truth remains that such is not fasting and is not required.

SUMMARY

When a fasting is not led by the Holy Spirit or is laid on the foundation of doubt or it begins and ends without prayer or is unconsciously observed, such fasting is simply not necessary

QUESTIONS

1. What if I don't hear the Holy Spirit can I still fast?

2. Must everyone fast since we can pray and achieve results (Luke 16 :10, Psalm 116 :17-18)

LESSON 5: RULES AND GUILDELINES ON FASTING

TEXT: Matthew 6:16-18 *Moreover when ye fast, be not, as the hypocrites, of a sad countenance: for they disfigure their faces, that they may appear unto men to fast. Verily I say unto you, They have their reward. But thou, when thou fastest, anoint thine head, and wash thy face; That thou appear not unto men to fast, but unto thy Father which is in secret: and thy Father, which seeth in secret, shall reward thee openly.*

MEMORY VERSE: Colossians 3:23 *And whatsoever ye do, do it heartily, as to the Lord, and not unto men;*

INTRODUCTION

For everything in life to go well certain rules regarding it must be observed especially when words to effectively fast, you must keep to certain rules and be conversant with the guidelines. This lesson focuses on rules out of be observed and the guild to fasting. The aim of this teaching is to impact believers who are struggling in understanding fasting as a result ignorant.

1. **FAST IN SECRET:** This does not mean to stay hidden in a secluded place but means not to be open to the public about what you are doing and how you are doing it. This is because it is a spiritual thing making it too obvious is described by Jesus as hypocrisy we don't need others to approve of us or hail us for fasting. God who sees in secret alone is the one we seek by our fasting. A very good way to keep your fasting secret is not to stay away from people because you are afraid of invitation to eat. You may directly declare it to those around you; be among

them and be effective in what you with them. There is no need lying to them when food is in involved. It is either you reject their offer or you postponed it till when your fasting will be over.

2. **BE DEVOTED**: Devotion is not a mere religious commitment but a spiritual action that that reveals your commitment and readiness to obtain whatever reason why you are fasting. When devotion is observed to the fullness there will never be room for irregularity such as sleeping, talking, watching movies, playing games and every order thing that has nothing to contribute to your spiritual life all in the name of passing time.

3. **SEPERATION:** Separation here means consecration; setting yourself aside from all forms of ungodliness, the things you say, the places you go to, the things you give attention to and the people you mingle with; make sure none

of them contaminate your spirit. (2 Corinthians 6:14-17)

4. **CONSIDER YOUR INTAKE OF FOOD AND WATER BEFORE AND AFTER THE FASTING:** For everyone who is fasting, this rule should never be overlooked in as much as fasting is a spiritual thing it has effect on the body. In order avoid constipation, stomach ache and other related health challenges resulting from fasting; you must consider how you eat and what you eat before and after fasting. It is recommended that you seek a professional advice on nutrition and balance diet and also orientations on quality eating habit.

SUMMARY

Rules play a big part in fasting. If the principles or recommendations provided here are followed, fasting can be efficient and rewarding

QUESTIONS

1. Mention the rules of effective fasting that you know

2. If fasting still effective if any of this rule is not observed

LESSON 6: TYPES OF FASTING

TEXT: Exodus 34:28 *And he was there with the LORD forty days and forty nights; he did neither eat bread, nor drink water. And he wrote upon the tables the words of the covenant, the ten commandments.*

MEMORY VERSE: Matthew 4:2 *And when he had fasted forty days and forty nights, he was afterward an hungred.*

INTRODUCTION

Fasting is a broad topic in Christianity; it is hard to discuss fasting without controversy especially as regard to how to fast and types of fasting. This is could be traced to denominational differences as well as individual misconception of the idea of fasting. This lesson teaches the types of fasting from a Biblical point of view as well as practical experience. The aim of this teaching is not add to existing controversies but to simplify the understanding process of the subject matter.

1. **COMPLETE FASTING:** This has nothing to do with timing or duration. It is complete because it involves total abstained from general intake e.g. food, water, drugs, juice, smoking etc not only has this got to do with intake but also everything abstainable in the discus of fasting. In Exodus 34:23 Mosses abstained from food and water on the mountain. In Matthew 4:2 Jesus also abstained from food

2. **PARTIAL FASTING:** This is not a less effective fasting compared to complete fasting. Rather it is partial because it involves a complete abstinence from certain food or drink. This is to say while observing partial fasting, foods, drink and activities can be taken or done but a particular food or drink even activity is totally abstained from. In Daniel 1: 12, Daniel observed a partial fast (Daniel 10: 3) this is also referred to as Daniel fast. They are many example of fasting in the bible that fall within this category.

3. **PRESCRIBED FAST**: This is not prescribed as in the ordinary sense of prescription because almost, if not all fasting come as prescriptions. Prescribed fast in this sense refers to a fast initiated by instruction. This kind of fast can be instructed either by the Holy Spirit, men of God or by yourself as a result of determination to overcome a particular problem of life. For example to overcome obsession of phone you can

prescribe a fast for yourself against the use of phone; or prescribe a restriction on what you do with your phone. That means throughout the stated time you won't touch the phone but use the time to glorify God.

SUMMARY

The concept of abstinence is what defines a type of fasting, not the length of the fast, whether it be forty days, twenty one days, three days, or the time six to six, six to three, or six to twelve. This is why the above-mentioned types of fasting are all concerned with what you abstain from.

QUESTIONS

1. What are the types of fasting you know?
2. Is there any difference between six to six and other lesser time fasting?

LESSON 7: SPIRITUAL OBLIGATIONS DURING FASTING

TEXT: Daniel 9:2-4 *In the first year of his reign I Daniel understood by books the number of the years, whereof the word of the LORD came to Jeremiah the prophet, that he would accomplish seventy years in the desolations of Jerusalem. And I set my face unto the Lord God, to seek by prayer and supplications, with fasting, and sackcloth, and ashes: And I prayed unto the LORD my God, and made my confession, and said, O Lord, the great and dreadful God, keeping the covenant and mercy to them that love him, and to them that keep his commandments;*

MEMORY VERSE: Daniel 9:3 *And I set my face unto the Lord God, to seek by prayer and supplications, with fasting, and sackcloth, and ashes:*

INTRODUCTION

No matter how long it lasts, fasting is ineffective when it solely involves abstinence. Instead, it works best when there are spiritual obligations involved. The spiritual obligations that must be upheld throughout the fasting process are taught in this lesson. The purpose of this teaching is to correct long-held misconceptions among believers that they had fasted when all they did during that time was work, watch movies, play video games, sleep, etc.

The following spiritual obligations are important for fasting to be successful:

1. **STUDY THE WORD OF GOD**: (John 6:63) fasting is a spiritual task as well as a journey of faith. This is why it should never go without studying the word God. The Bible contains God's words, voice, promises, instructions, blessings and many more which is exactly the reason why we are fasting

2. **MEDITATION:** (Joshua 1:8, psalm 1:3-5) meditation is a very necessary practice during

fasting. Rather than pacing around in order to succumb the existing hunger spending time in meditation can give you access to a massive wealth of knowledge and deeper spiritual encounter. If for nothing spare a period of your fasting time to reflect on your life.

3. **WORSHIP:** When worship is mentioned the picture painted is usually that of singing. However, this goes beyond singing alone spending time talking with God, in surrendership, acknowledge his greatness and lordship over your life.

4. **PRAYING**: It is called fasting and prayers because the two are separate though are inter woven. Prayer can go without fasting but fasting cannot with prayer. Spending time in prayer during fasting is worth more than doing other things.

5. **LIVE RIGHT AND DO CHARITY WORKS:** Help those in needs, counsel people rightly live

exemplary life and be careful of defiling or ruining the fast your have started.

SUMMARY

The following spiritual obligations must be met when fasting: Studying the Bible, praying, worshiping, living righteously, and doing charity works.

QUESTIONS:

1. Mention the spiritual obligations that must be when fasting

2. Can one fast without performing some of these spiritual obligations mentioned?

LESSON 8: HOW OFTEN SHOULD WE FAST?

TEXT: LUKE 5:33-35 *And they said unto him, Why*

do the disciples of John fast often, and make prayers, and likewise the disciples of the Pharisees; but thine eat and drink? And he said unto them, Can ye make the children of the bride chamber fast, while the bridegroom is with them? But the days will come, when the bridegroom shall be taken away from them, and then shall they fast in those days.

MEMORY VERSE: MARK 9:29 *And he said unto them, This kind can come forth by nothing, but by prayer and fasting.*

INTROUDUCTION

When it pertains to fasting especially how often a Christian should fast, a lot of Christians are confused, some a result have considered fasting a routine that they don't eat or drink at a given period of the year, month or week. While there are many who have habitually forsaken breakfast in the name of fasting, there are Christians who hardly fast at all for reasons good for them alone. There is a need to understand how often a Christian should fast even though the Bible does not say anything directly regarding it. This lesson explains how frequently Christians should fast. In an effort to correct, the lesson's goal is to inform and enlighten.

1. **AS OFTEN AS THE SPIRIT LEADS:** Jesus was lead by the spirit onto fasting (Matthew 4:1); Elijah having been fed by the angel got strength to fast (1 kings 19:8) When it has to do with fasting the Spirit of God must be involved. And no matter what, you are to fast as often as the Spirit leads. He the spirit will give you the strength necessary and guide you through as you obey His leading.

2. **AS OFTEN AS YOUR LOCAL CHURCH OR PASTOR PRESCRIBES**: the church is the body of Christ and Jesus is the head. He leads his church through the pastors or other named leader. Therefore as often as your pastor or leaders propose a fast, obey for it is same as the

Spirits leading. Esther, the Apostles, the king of Nineveh etc all proposed fasting to their followers in the Bible.

3. **AS OFTEN AS YOU NOTICE THE NEED FOR REVIVAL OR REPENTANCE**: Going into fasting is very recommendable when in need for revival or repentance. David, the people of Nineveh, and many others in the Bible are examples for us to learn from Therefore as often as you notice in your life the need for revival, spiritual fire is getting weak it is recommended that you fast. If you also seek perfect repentance, it recommended that you fast.

4. AS OFTEN AS CONDITIONS CAUSE THE NEED TO FAST: Jesus explained to his disciples that some spiritual and physical issues cannot be resolved without fasting and prayer. You should always pray, but if the situation calls for fasting, do not delay. (Mark 9:29)

SUUMMARY

We ought to fast as often as the Spirit leads, church proposed necessity warranted or as often as you seek to put on spiritual weight keeping the fire in you burning or surrendering before the lord for mercy rather than believing it is ideal to fast regularly for repentance and for spiritual fire, it is advisable instead that you keep off from sin and never allow the fire in you to quench. Eat and save your strength for when your church or the Holy Spirit will propose a fast to you or when you must doggedly change the condition of things through prayer and fasting.

QUESTION

1. How do you know when the Spirit is leading you to fast?
2. How often do you fast in a year/why?
3. How often should Christians fast?

LESSON 9: SOME REASONS WHY MANY CHRISTIANS DON'T FAST

TEXT: 1 Corinthians 3:1-3 *And I, brethren, could not speak unto you as unto spiritual, but as unto carnal, even as unto babes in Christ. I have fed you with milk, and not with meat: for hitherto ye were not able to bear it, neither yet now are ye able. For ye are yet carnal: for whereas there is among you envying, and strife, and divisions, are ye not carnal, and walk as men?*

MEMORY VERSE: 1 Corinthians 2:14 *But the natural man receiveth not the things of the Spirit of God: for they are foolishness unto him: neither can he know them, because they are spiritually discerned.*

INTRODUCTION

Many Christians do not fast at all or may only fast sometimes, despite hearing about fasting and prayer. This lesson explains the reasons for this.

Here are some explanations why so many eligible and healthy Christians don't fast.

1. **SPIRITUAL IMMATURITY**: This has summed up many different reasons put together. In as much as fasting is physically not for babies it is spiritually the same not for spiritual babies. It is a discipline for grownups. As a problem, the symptoms are excuses, fear of ulcer and other hunger related sickness, laziness, additions and obsessions. Of course a baby cannot stay without food but a grow up can. If you come across anyone who those not fast whatever excuse he or she may provide is covered by the fact that he or she is still a spiritual baby. Such people can be transformed only by a close nurturing.

2. **POOR SPIRITUAL UPBRINGING:** This problem can be attributed to poor parenting both

relating to biological parents and spiritual leaders. It will be difficult to find yourself into fasting as other Christians do if you have a poor spiritual upbringing. Parents are suppose to play the role of grooming their children in the ways of the Lord and this should have to start from childhood stage otherwise the child will grow without it. A study of denominationalism has proven also that there are denominations that pay less or no attention to fasting. In such places all that the spiritual fathers can raise up may never see fasting the way other Christians do and would never fast. Some unfiltered doctrines are really to blame for this.

3. **LUKE-WARMNESS:** When a believer gets cold or lacks fire, every other spiritual thing will cease to have meaning before him. Being a pastor, prayer warrior or any strong title that suggest your depth in the Lord does not count and can change nothing, except the fire is restored back

and this will take only a great revival involving fasting and prayers.

4. **LACK OF FAITH:** Whether you are a spiritual adult, well brought up still under fire, if you lack adequate faith in fasting, you will never see reasons why you should fast. Some people in the category instead of having faith fear that something wrong may happen to their health if they fast so they prefer to pray continually and not fast no matter the circumstances they will not surrender even if the Holy Spirit proposes fasting to them such people don't produce much result in their spiritual race.

SUMMARY

Spiritual immaturity, poor spiritual foundation/upbringing, luke-warmness and lack of faith are the reasons why many eligible and healthy Christians don't fast. The remedy to all these is submission and revival.

QUESTIONS

1. Mention any three reasons why you think some Christians do not fast

2. Must every Christian fast?

CHAPTER TWO: DOUBT

LESSON 1: REASONS WHY PEOPLE DOUBT GOD

TEXT: James 1:6 *But let him ask in faith, nothing wavering. For he that wavereth is like a wave of the sea driven with the wind and tossed. For let not that man think that he shall receive any thing of the Lord. A double minded man is unstable in all his ways.*

MEMORY VERSE: James 1:8 *A double minded man is unstable in all his ways.*

INTRODUCTION

Doubt is the opposite of faith. It is another word for unbelief. Christianity is all about faith and nothing less than that but unfortunately there are many Christians who don't believe. They claim they do but they harbor doubts in them. This lesson reveals why this is so and is aimed at correction

1. **WHEN THE EXPECTED TIME OF DELIVERY HAS ELAPSE**: (Genesis 17:17- 22) Sarah the wife of Abraham doubted God when she has gone past the age of childbearing; that she laughed when it was prophesied that she will give birth. Likewise Zachariah the priest and father to John the Baptist. He questioned the angel out of his doubt because he was also very old. (Luke 1:18). Many people today doubt God over many things and the reason is because they have gone past their time of the expectation.

2. **FEAR:** the Israelites including Gideon had been living for several years in great fear of their enemies the Medianites. As a result Gideon doubted the angel who came with message of victory to him. He delayed the angel by asking multiple questions and doubted even when the angle was assuring him of victory (Judges 6:36).

Peter the chief disciple of Jesus once walked upon water alongside Jesus but he sank when he began to entertain fear of the strong wind. Fear is another opposite of faith; anytime it is entertained, faith disappears and that is doubt.

3. **WALKING BY SIGHT:** There are the people who believe in the principle of "seeing is believing". Thomas one of the disciples of Jesus is a good example of this kind of people he said until 'I see I can't believe' (John 20:24:25). This principle is quite good for life and business but not for Christianity for Christianity is a move of faith and the wisdom of the world cannot be substituted for that of the kingdom of God. The children do not walk by sight but by faith. If anyone walks by sight he or she would have to doubt God and never receive from God. Can an army of three hundred fighters prevail over tens of thousands? Can five loaves of bread and two fishes be sufficient enough to feed five thousand

persons? Can water filled in jars be substitutes for wine in an occasion? Not at all. All these can't be if sight should decide. But by faith all became possible in. Judges 7:4-25, John 6:6-12 and John 2:7-11 respectfully. Many people doubt because they believe certain things are impossible and difficult to archive (2kings 7:1:2). The king's official response to Elisha shows his doubt because he thought it is impossible for a famine that lasted for years to end up in day and for food to be as cheap as Elisha described. Remember Jesus' response in (Mark 10:27) *all things are possible with God.*

4. **FAMILIARITY**: (Mark 6: 4:5) the people of His home town where too familiar with, Jesus that they doubted His anointing and as a result, there was little or no miracle at all because Jesus couldn't perform.(2 chronicle 20:20) getting familiar with things and people in life has its own disadvantages. They could make you lose faith or doubt easily. For instance, when you

become too familiar a prophet, a way of prayer, a place of prayer etc you could shift your believe on them too easily especially when greater wind of troubles blows. Some people don't believe in the power of God's word hidden in certain scriptures simply because they have memorizes and therefore have become familiar with them. Familiarity can lead to doubts.

SUMMARY

Doubt is never supposed to have been seen among believers because the essence of our believe is that we have grown past doubt. For whatever reason is a believer doubts God he is no longer a believer but an unbeliever. This is why the bible says, it is impossible to please God without faith. Hebrews 11:6

QUESTIONS

1. Mention some reasons why many people doubt God

2. Can familiarity to scripture cause doubt? Explain how.

LESSON 2: CONSEQUENCE OF DOUBTING GOD

TEXT: Luk 1:19-21 *And the angel answering said unto him, I am Gabriel, that stand in the presence of God; and am sent to speak unto thee, and to shew thee these glad tidings. And, behold, thou shalt be dumb, and not able to speak, until the day that these things shall be performed, because thou believest not my words, which shall be fulfilled in their season. And the people waited for Zacharias, and marveled that he tarried so long in the temple.*

MEMORY VERSE: James 1:6 *But let him ask in faith, nothing wavering. For he that wavereth is like a wave of the sea driven with the wind and tossed. For let not that man think that he shall* *receive any thing of the Lord.*

INTRODUCTION

Like faith, living doubt also has its own effects or consequences. This lesson reveals the underlying effects or the consequences of doubting God.

The consequences of doubting god are:

1. **IT HINDERS THE MIRACULOUS FLOW GODS POWER:** (Mark 6: 4:5 see how Jesus couldn't perform any sign in His own town because the people doubted Him. David in 1 Samuel 17:28-30 would have been withheld from killing Goliath and becoming the hero of the Israelites if he had listened to his brother. For any reason no one should doubt God because it can limit the move of God. This does not mean that God's power is limited but rather that God withhold His glory from anyone who doubts Him.

2. **IT BRINGS AFFLICTION ON THE PEOPLE** (Luke 1:18:19) Zachariah the priest was afflicted with dumbness as a result of his doubt to the message of angle Gabriel.

3. **IT CAN CAUSE DEATH**: The king's official in 2Kings 7:1-2 doubted the prophetic words of Elisha and as a result faced the consequence as the prophet prophesied in verse 19 and 20 the same chapter. In 1 Samuel 17:45-51, Goliath the warrior of the Philistines not only dared the Israelites and insulted Jehovah; he also doubted God's capability of using David as a result, he payed with him life. This is the same with the other at the other hand of Jesus on the cross. He doubted and spoke against Jesus with his last breathe. We are sure he will never spend eternity near Jesus unlike his colleague. He signed up for eternal death. This is still applicable today and unless we replace our doubt with faith similar fate might await us.

4. **IT LEADS TO SIN AS SIN IS REBELLION AGAINST GOD** (Romans 14:23). Doubt is the opposite of faith. Therefore the bible said anything not faith is sin. ***But without faith it is impossible to please him: for he that cometh to God must believe that he is, and that he is a rewarder of them that diligently seek him. Hebrews 11:6***

5. **IT LIMITS PROGRESS IN LIFE**: Peter was walking on the water with Jesus and he began to sink when he doubted. Many today are sinking in life because he began to doubt God (Matthew 14:22:36). If you are looking for reasons why many people are stranded in life; consider this.

SUMMARY

The consequences of doubts are practically numerous and unstoppable compared to the doubt and the reasons for doubting God. If you are in the category of people who constantly express doubts against God's words or doubt God in any form, consider this.

QUESTIONS

1. What are the consequences of doubting God?
2. How can one avoid these consequences?

LESSON 3: HOW TO OVERCOME DOUBTS

TEXT: James 4:7 *Submit yourselves therefore to God. Resist the devil, and he will flee from you.*

MEMORY VERSE: James 1:6 *But let him ask in faith, nothing wavering. For he that wavereth is like a wave of the sea driven with the wind and tossed.*

INTRODUCTION

This lesson reveals how to overcome doubts. It is essential for every child of God to master the act of overcoming doubts because without faith it is practically impossible to work with God.

1. **THINK BEYOND THE PRESENTED FEAR**; in (Matthew 14: 22-36), Peter sank into the water when he began to nurture the fear of sinking. Mary and Martha in (John 11) couldn't have doubted Jesus that they were not thinking of the presented fear that Lazarus had been buried for four days. We can overcome doubt if we look beyond the fear (2 Corinthians 5:7) "we walk by faith not by sight"

2. **STOP DOUBTING TAKE ACTION**: Mary the mother of Jesus in John 2:5 said to the men in the wedding at Cana " *do whatever He asked you to do*" other disciple were still doubting when peter joined Jesus to walk on the sea. It was easy for Peter because he overcame his doubt by taking action (James 2:26)

3. **REMEMBER THE TESTIMONIES OF GODS GREATNESS**. (Psalm 77:11). David as a boy in 1 Samuel 17: 33-37 went into the battle with Goliath without a doubt of the victory God will grant him. This was because he remembered his past victories over lion and bear with God by his side.

4. **ASK GOD FOR HELP:** GOD can help us to overcome doubt. The father of the demon possessed boy in (Mark 9:24) asked Jesus to help him overcome doubt. *Note; everything is possible with god.*

5. **LIVE BY FAITH:** (Galatians 3:11) we will permanently overcome doubt if we live our life in faith. All things work for good to them who are called according to His purpose. Those whom God love .for without faith no one can please God

SUMMARY

Doubt can be overcome like every other work of Satan. Following all the above mentioned, it is also very expedient to equip yourself with the word of God. These are basic information which has to do what who God is, how much He love you and how much He has said the promised you.

QUESTIONS

1. Mention how you can overcome doubts
2. How can studying the word of God help you to overcome doubt?

LESSON 4: BENEFITS OF NOT DOUBTING GOD

TEXT: *Ask, and it shall be given you; seek, and ye shall find; knock, and it shall be opened unto you:*

MEMORY VERSE: Mark 11:24 *Therefore I say unto you, What things soever ye desire, when ye pray,* *believe that ye receive them, and ye shall have them.*

INTRODUCTION

Believing God and never doubting Him is indeed beneficial. This lesson reveals some of the benefits which come to it.

1. **MIRACLES:** Jesus turned water into wine at Galilee (John 2) Jesus raised Lazarus from death (John 11) By Jesus' instruction peter cut multitude of fish etc.(john 21) all these and many more happened because the atmosphere was without doubt. Anyone who in God without doubting is bound to receive miracles.

2. **RECEIVING FROM GOD:** (Matthew 21:22) whenever we pray and not doubt we will receive from God in Mark 5:25, the unnamed woman with issue of blood got what she prayed for because she never doubted. Hannah the mother of Samuel, Hezekiah, Jabest etc are among many who prayed and received from God because they never doubted.

3. **HEALING:** is one of the benefit of not doubting in Mark 1: 40, a leaper came to Jesus full of believe and he got cured in Mark 2:1-12 four men carried their paralytic friend to Jesus full of believe they dropped him right before Jesus through an open roof; he got cured because of his friends faith. In Matthew 15:28, Jesus healed the daughter of a Canaanite woman ascribing that the healing happened because the woman had a great faith. The book of James 5:15 says, a prayer of faith can heal the sick.

4. **DIVINE PROTECTION:** God's protections are guaranteed to anyone who believes and not doubt God. King David in Psalm 23, 91, 27, and many other chapters of Psalm emphasized how much he had confidence of God's protections over his life because he believes.

Yea, though I walk through the valley of the shadow of death, I will fear no evil: for thou art with me; thy rod and thy staff they comfort me psalm 23:4

The LORD is my light and my salvation; whom shall I fear? the LORD is the strength of my life; of whom shall I be afraid? When the wicked, even mine enemies and my foes, came upon me to eat up my flesh, they stumbled and fell. Though an host should encamp against me, my heart shall not fear: though war should rise against me, in this will I be confident. Psalm 27:1-3

I will say of the LORD, He is my refuge and my fortress: my God; in him will I trust. Surely he shall deliver thee from the snare of the fowler, and from the noisome pestilence. He shall cover thee with his feathers, and under his wings shalt thou trust: his truth shall be thy shield and buckler. Thou shalt not be afraid for the terror by night; nor for the arrow that flieth by day; Nor for the pestilence that walketh in darkness; nor for the destruction that wasteth at noonday. A thousand shall fall at thy side, and ten thousand at thy right hand; but it shall not come nigh thee. Only with thine eyes shalt thou behold and see the reward of the wicked. Psalm 91:2-8

SUMMARY

Beyond those mentioned above, there are many more benefits of trusting in God instead of doubts. This is a practical lesson that should always be given attention because everyone who practice trust in God would certainly experience the same benefits.

QUESTIONS

1. Mention the benefits of not doubting God you know

2. Is it possible to enjoy these benefits on the account of someone else's faith?

CHAPTER THREE: SERVICE TO GOD

LESSON 1: SERVING GOD

TEXT: John 12:26 *If any man serve me, let him follow me; and where I am, there shall also my servant be: if any man serve me, him will my Father honour.*

MEMORY VERSE: Joshua 24:15 *And if it seem evil unto you to serve the LORD, choose you this day whom ye will serve; whether the gods which your fathers served that were on the other side of the flood, or the gods of the Amorites, in whose land ye dwell: but as for me and my house, we will serve the LORD.*

INTRODUCTION

Serving is an act of pleasing a person and this can be done in many ways and for multiple reasons and mentionable benefits. Every child of God ought to understand what it means to serve God. This lessons, teaches why we must serve God.

WHY WE SERVE GOD

1. **ITS GOD'S WILL FOR US; FOR WE ARE CREATED TO SERVE**: We are all created and called to serve God. (Genesis 1:27-28) God made man in his image and likeness which suggest that like God, man is made with the ability to serve and to be served. (MARK 10:45 Jesus indicated that son of man has come to serve and not to be served). God after the creation of Adam first put him in the Garden of Eden to serve. Jesus while ascending to heaven charged us to serve God (Matthew 28:19-20); Holy Spirit give gifts and fruits to men in order to equip them all for the purpose of serving God. We are created to please the lord by serving him in all ways.

2. **TO HONOUR GOD**: (Malachi 1:6) God is our maker. Does he not deserve the place of a father

and great master in our lives? Indeed he does and this is why we must serve him more than we can.

3. **IT IS COMMAND**: (1 Samuel 12:24, Exodus 20:2-4) It is a great command to serve God our maker; therefore we must serve him

4. **WE ARE GOD'S INSTRUMENTS**: (Acts 9:15) Serving God shouldn't be considered a big deal among us the children of God; because we are his instruments. And can do nothing except by his making.

5. **WE SHALL GIVE ACCOUNT OF WHAT WE DO:** (Romans 14: 12) If for all other aforementioned reason we don't serve God, we are to consider this single most serious reason why we must serve God. We shall face judgment after death and our works shall be counted.

SUMMARY

Serving God should have no limitations. It is for everyone regardless of age or gender and the reasons for this are just the aforementioned.

QUESTIONS

1. What does it mean to serve God?
2. Mention two reasons why we serve God

LESSON 2: QUALITIES NECESSARY FOR SERVING GOD

TEXT: MATTHEW 16:24 *Then said Jesus unto his disciples, If any man will come after me, let him deny himself, and take up his cross, and follow me.*

MEMORY VERSE: 2 TIMONTHY 3:12 *Yea, and all that will live godly in Christ Jesus shall suffer persecution.*

INTRODUCTION

As there certain qualities you must exhibit in order to be successful in life, so also are there qualities you must acquire in order to serve God efficiently. Our earlier studies have shown why we must serve God; this study will explain how we can serve God by highlighting certain qualities which we must possess in order to serve God efficiently. Biblically and practically, it has been demonstrated that no one can serve God effectively and for a very long time without displaying these characteristics:

1. **DETEREMINATION AND ZEAL**: (Psalm 69:7-9, Rev 3:19); Determination is very necessary because without it no one can ever make a decision to serve God. It takes zeal to maintain determination. When you come across people who serve God with zeal; however determined they are to serve God, they will be struggling in it. The disciples of Jesus were determined to serve but their zeal was fluctuating. Until they

got empowered by the Holy Spirit. If you find a zealous person whose zeal is founded on his or her determination whatever he does, he will do well.

2. **LOYALTY AND DELIGENCE:** (Rom 12:11, 1 chronicles 16:11). Loyalty is an absolute display of truthfulness and submission. It is borne by determination to serve and sustained by zeal. Diligence likewise is a commitment to doing it right without missing it from any side. Put together both diligence and loyalties are qualities that should never be lacking in our service to God. (It takes a degree of loyalty to be diligent).

3. **PATIENCE AND ENDURANCE:** (Psalm 27:14, Rom 12:12). These two are not the same though they are often confused to be same. Patience is waiting in great trust while endurance is bearing the pains in the process of waiting. The two often work hand in hand. You can distinguish endurance from patience when especially you

have everything life offers and needed nothing or except nothing but have a burden to bear which cannot be solved, (Psalm 86:11, Galatians 6:9, Luke 14:27); by your riches. You will come across many burdens you will only rely on God to lift up from your head.

4. **JOY:** This is a feeling that is beyond happiness and is necessary when serving God. It is an absolver of pains and all other trials that may arise. It is necessary to serve God with great joy.

5. **HUMULITY**: This is the absence of pride. As well as the near opposite of pomposity. Without this quality, it will be difficult to serve God. Serving God provides platform for a test of humility. Lucifer failed because he lacks complete humility. (Isaiah 14:12-15)

SUMMARY

Many will propose that the first quality needed to serving God is love, this is true but it cannot be shown without all these mentioned above.

Jesus said if you love me, keep my commandments. Yes but all these mentioned above are necessary if the commandment must be kept.

QUESTIONS

1. Mention any three qualities required for serving God efficiently
2. Do all Christians posses these qualities?

LESSON 3: BENEFITS OF SERVING GOD

TEXT: *EXODUS 23:25-28 And ye shall serve the LORD your God, and he shall bless thy bread, and thy water; and I will take sickness away from the midst of thee. There shall nothing cast their young, nor be barren, in thy land: the number of thy days I will fulfil. I will send my fear before thee, and will destroy all the people to whom thou shalt come, and I will make all thine enemies turn their backs unto thee. And I will send hornets before thee, which shall drive out the Hivite, the Canaanite, and the Hittite, from before thee.*

MEMORY VERSE: HEBREWS 11: 6 *But without faith it is impossible to please him: for he that cometh to God must believe that he is, and that he is a rewarder of them that diligently seek him.*

INTRODUCTION

God is greatly benevolent. He rewards those who seek him. This lesson teaches the rewards or benefit in serving God.

Here are the rewards or the benefits to enjoy when serving God:

1. **ENJOY HIS PROVISIONS WITHOUT STUGGLING**: (Matthew 6:33-34) you will enjoy God's provision without toiling if you serve God,

as He promised in His words. The bible is full of such related promises. (Psalm 127:3, 121)

2. **DIVINE PROTECTION**: God will never let any harm befall those who serve Him. Here are some scriptures for this. (Psalm 105:15, 1 chronicles 16:22), etc. In Genesis 20:7 and Exodus 22:28 among others, God responded against those who dare to harm His servants.

3. **HONOUR:** (1 Samuel 2:30). Those who serve God are honored by Him. Many biblical figures, including Samuel, Moses, Elijah, and others, were accorded such honor by God that, like immortals, neither their words nor their deeds were fruitless. Until they reached the Promised Land and lived triumphant lives there, God honored the Israelites with victories wherever they went, making their enemies extremely terrified by them. He honored Jesus, Joseph, Esther, Mordecai, and all others who served Him.

4. **GOOD HEALTH AND LONG LIFE**: (Exodus 23:25-28); living healthy and dying in good old age is one great benefit that God gives those who serve Him. Moses, Abraham etc. were healthy and strong till death in a good old age.

5. **JOY AND PEACE OF MIND:** (Psalms 127:3); in the midst of great chaos and daily life problems God does not forsake those who serve him. In one way or the other God ensures peace of mind for his.

6. **ENJOY SPIRITUAL GIFTS**: (Ephesians 4:11-12) God gives plenty spiritual gifts to those who serve him. All these gifts are meant to make life and God's work easier. The gifts turn men into spiritual beings.

7. **SERVICE TO GOD ADVANCES GOD'S KINGDOM:** (Zachariah 1:17) this is very true because the kingdom of God advances further easily when men are serving. There are many functioning departments in the church where services are required. If only brethren will avail

themselves, the kingdom will great advance beyond the walls of the earth.

SUMMARYS

God is indeed good and faithful to His promises. If only we can serve God which is our commitment, we stand to benefit from mentioned above.

QUESTIONS

1. Mention all the benefits of serving God?
2. Have you ever seen anyone serving God without enjoying these benefits?

LESSON 4: THE CHALLENGES OF SERVING GOD

TEXT: 1 Corinthians 10:13 *There hath no temptation taken you but such as is common to man: but God is* *faithful, who will not suffer you to be tempted above that ye are able; but will with the temptation also make a way to escape, that ye may be able to bear it.*

MEMORY VERSE: Luke 9:23 *And he said to them all, If any man will come after me, let him deny himself, and take up his cross daily, and follow me.*

INTRODUCTION

Beyond every other aspect of life, serving God also has its own challenges. This lesson not only mentions these challenges but also reveals their sources.

Here are the challenges of serving God:

1. **SATAN:** (Revelation 12:10; 16-17, John 10:10). He is neither an opposite nor opposition to God but to men. He sinned from the beginning and lost his estate casted out of heaven. He is out here to wage war against the children of God to ensure

that they are casted into hell along with him. Satan is the chief challenge every servant or follower of God has. He is restless until he brings his targets down (1 peter 5:8). There are many ways in which Satan challenges the children of God they are:

a. **TEMPTATION**: This is a trap of Satan meant to hook down children of God into regret, stagnation, lack, untold suffering and diverse misery. This begins by an attraction then ends in sin. As a trap Satan uses diverse attractive things to bait or lure children of God into sin. Knowing that sin violates holiness and unholiness is detachment from the Lord. Satan uses temptation to demote, kill and excommunicate a child of God from God's presence. Every child of God who wishes to committedly serve God is automatically a target of Satan. Therefore he or she must live to the challenge of resisting the devil throughout their life time. It's a big challenge indeed. Jesus, David, Solomon and many others experienced it in the Bible.

b. **TRIALS:** (1 peter 1:7; James 1:2-3) this is often confused to be temptation but is not. The difference is, while temptation aims at luring and dragging you into sin, trial is a season of unavoidable problems not necessarily created by you. Satan is quite behind trials although in this case he is permitted by God. The purpose of trails is similar to that of school quiz or examination. It proves your faith and decision to serving the Lord. Elijah, Job, Joseph and many others experienced this in the Bible. Note as a child of God trial will always come and this is to challenge your faith. Hardships, loss, failures, afflictions and other diverse nameless and namable problems of life are examples of trials.

c. **PERSECUTION:** (Matthew 5:11-12)   Satan opposes a child of God through persecution, here he can influence, manipulate, or by any means entice people to persecute you. Persecution is a direct attack against your faith or service to God. It can take the form of decrees if the authorities are used, or culture, family tradition, accusation etc. This could end up in death, prison, assaults, damage, mob attacks, kidnappings and others. When you see these things, do not give up rather see that it is only a challenge and God will show you the way out of it.

2. **GOD**: (Genesis 22: 1) Serving God means pleasing Him. God is a super being whose ways are beyond our comprehension except they are revealed to us. God Himself poses a challenge to those who are serving Him and the way He does this is through a test. God tests our obedience, patience, endurance, love for Him and others. This test might come in unexpected ways (forgiving one another, helping the needy, following hard instructions, praying for a particular issue without result and all other

scenarios) are all challenges in serving God which God himself posses on us. (Matthew 25:40)

3. **SPIRIT VS FLESH**: The spirit is always contrary to the flesh. Serving God is entire a spiritual thing however, the spirit needs the flesh because it housed in it. Therefore the challenge of submitting the flesh to the spirit must be given due attention. The two conflict in strength, choice and needs. Jesus seeks to make us understand this very well when He said the spirit is willing but flesh is weak.

SUMMARY

Serving God is indeed not without its challenges: while Satan attacks through temptations, trials and persecutions, standing the tests from God Himself, and facing the combat between our spirit and body are all challenges every Christian must prepare to face and overcome them.

QUESTIONS

1. What are the challenges of serving God?

2. Why would God Himself permit or approve of problems to come on His people?

LESSON 5: SOME REASONS WHY PEOPLE DON'T SERVE GOD

TEXT: Matthew 19:21 *Jesus said unto him, If thou wilt be perfect, go and sell that thou hast, and give to the poor, and thou shalt have treasure in heaven: and come and follow me.*

MEMORY VERSE: Ecclesiastes 12:1 *Remember now thy Creator in the days of thy youth, while the evil days come not, nor the years draw nigh, when thou shalt say, I have no pleasure in them;*

INTRODUCTION: This lesson reveals some reasons why many people do not serve God.

1. **DOUBT**: (James 1: 6-8). There are still people who doubt everything about God. His existence, His word and His followers. Some of these doubts could be as a result of personal experiences and other related problems.

2. **LOVE FOR THE WORLD**: (Galatians 5:5-16). There are people who don't serve God because they love the things of the world and cannot go spiritual and forget carnality. This people centered their lives on the carnal things. Jesus says no one can serve two masters.

3. **THEY ARE DECEIVED BY THE DEVIL**: (Revelation 12:9) many such in this category have been deceived by the devil to believe that there are better ways of living apart from serving God. Such are people who speak like these: not all are called to serve God, Angels are enough and capable to serve God why we? We go to church only for ceremony- church is in the heart- serving God is excuse for laziness and failure etc.

4. **WRONG UPBRINGING**: (Proverbs 22:6). Some among this category actually would have serve God and done better but they have poor spiritual fathers, poor spiritual foundation ancestral backgrounds.

SUMMARY

Child of God needs to see the need for evangelism by this alone in order to address his big issue.

QUESTIONS

1. What are the reasons why people don't serve God?

2. Explain how the Devil deceives people

CHAPTER FOUR: DEATH

LESSON 1: ORIGIN OF DEATH AND WHY PEOPLE DIE

TEXT: GENESIS 2:17 *But of the tree of the knowledge of good and evil, thou shalt not eat of it: for in the day that thou eatest thereof thou shalt surely die.*

MEMORY VERSE: HEBREWS 9:27 *And as it is appointed unto men once to die, but after this the judgment:*

INTRODUCTION

When it comes to the issue of death, everyone is curious. But the truth is there are details about death that we cannot access as mortals especially while we live. No matter how limited we are in this regards, there are more to say and learn. This lesson reveals the origin of death as well as the reason why people die.

THE ORIGIN OF DEATH

Death is the inexistence of life, the very end of existence in one realm and transition into another realm. Death was originated by sin incited by Satan at the Garden of Eden. The story of Adam and Eve (Genesis 3:1-24). Prior to the fall or spiritual death of Adam and Eve, some events had taken place in Heaven which led to the death of some angels. From among whom is Lucifer now popular as the Devil or Satan. He brought death to mankind through Adam and Eve. God had never pronounced death on mankind, but He will one-day do so to all who follow the devil on the judgment day.

THE REASONS OR CAUSES OF DEATH

1. **SIN**: As we already have seen in the case of Adam and Eve; sin still causes spiritual death, as seen in the case of Eli, (1 Sam 4), Korah and the

72 (Numbers 16:20-25), king Herod (Acts 12). Sin also causes physical death and eternal death as in the case of Satan and his demons.

2. **CARELESSNESS**: This also causes death. A man called Eutichus died on the spot where Apostle Paul was preaching. (Acts 20:9) he was so careless not to have noticed where he sat to listen to the teachings he fell while asleep.

3. **IGNORANCE:** This as seen in the Bible can kill till today. Elijah killed 102 army of the king by calling fire to consume them (1Kings 18: 38). These men are ignorant of the capabilities of the prophet by the power of God upon him. Likewise the prophets of Baal (1 Kings 18: 19-29), the sons of prophets who mocked Elisha (2 Kings 2:24), the young prophets in (1king 13: 23-26) and many others. Many people today are death because of ignorance. Failure to know what you should know is still killing many people in many aspects especially ignorance in health tips.

4. **ACCIDENTS:** (Ecclesiastes 10:9). This is usually unforeseen, though it's often attributed to carelessness, accidents cause death. In our world now, accident is one of the major causes of death.

5. **SICKNESS:** Our body is made up of many systems which put together must be healthy to be active. Sickness is any malfunction in health condition. It is one of the major causes of death in the Bible and today.

6. **WAR/FIGHT**: Following provocation, war or fighting can easily lead to death. The Bible has many records of fight battles which led to the death of many. Today we see riots, fights, rubbery attacks etc.

7. **OLD AGE/WHEN TIME TO DIE:** (Ecclesiastes 3:1-5). As the Bible says, there it time for everything. This includes the time to die. Indeed death awaits every mortal here on earth except those that will be ruptured. Therefore time for

death is generally at elapse of good old age or when time is reached.

SUMMARY

These mentioned causes of death, have been in vogue from the beginning of mortal death till now. Believers are not to fear for anything apart from sin for none of these can overtake a child of God.

QUESTIONS

1. Account for the origin of mortal death
2. Mention any three cause of death studied in this lesson

LESSON 2: TYPES OF DEATH

TEXT: Revelation 21:8 *But the fearful, and unbelieving, and the abominable, and murderers, and whoremongers, and sorcerers, and idolaters, and all liars, shall have their part in the lake which burneth with fire and brimstone: which is the second death.*

MEMORY VERSE: Philippians 1:21 *For to me to live is Christ, and to die is gain.*

INTRODUCTION: How is it possible to say or believe that there are many kinds of death? Of course they should be: because man lives in the body but also has a soul and a spirit .if the death known to us only takes the body, then there ought to be other death aside from the one we know. This lesson teaches three types of death –this is to inform believers so that they will learn to worry little over the physical death and pay more attention the other deaths.

THREE TYPES OF DEATH

1. **THE SPIRITUAL DEATH:** (Genesis 2:17), this is the death which God was speaking about to Adam. It is not actually a physical death. This death means extinction of the spirit or simply to imply the separation from the spirit of God. Satan who himself had died of this kind of death from the beginning; Knew what it meant but went ahead to deceive the woman Eve in the garden (Genesis 3:4). This kind of death can come anytime. Although Jesus had delivered mankind from the forceful grip of this kind of death-today many believers willingly give in to this kind of death by accepting sin and forsaking God.

2. **THE PHYSICAL DEATH:** This is the one everyone knows and calls death. Since the origin of death, man not only lost his spirit to Satan but

also lost his mortality which limited the life span of mankind. When this kind of death occurs, the body fades away but the spirit and soul remain.

3. **THE ETERNAL DEATH:** This is referred to as the second death in the Bible. This is the death which Satan, his demons and all who have followed Satan will die in the fire of hell. It is eternal in the sense that it has no end. Believers consider this death to be once because Christ Jesus has died to free us from sin which is the signature to eternal death. Once we align ourselves with the finish works of Jesus, we have only one death to die.

SUMMARY

The study of these types of death has nothing to add to a believer, reason being that Jesus has over powered death for us; and has liked us to eternal life though we will die the physical death, like Jesus it is only a sleep for we will resurrect one day when Jesus calls; and there after live everly happy with him as saints. Satan would not let this be to us so easy as it may sound. He will continue to try us like Adam and Eve to lure into his den of death. So this teaching is relevant to us in that it remind us of the evil that will befall us when we give in to Satan's deception.

QUESTIONS

1. Mention the three types of death
2. Will everyone die these three times?
3. Explain how we die spiritually?
4. How did Jesus over power death for us?

LESSON 3: HOW TO AVOID SPIRITUAL AND ETERNAL DEATH.

TEXT: Acts 16:29-31 *Then he called for a light, and sprang in, and came trembling, and fell down before*

Paul and Silas, And brought them out, and said, Sirs, what must I do to be saved? And they said, Believe on the Lord Jesus Christ, and thou shalt be saved, and thy house.

MEMEORY VERSE: Romans 10:9 *That if thou shalt confess with thy mouth the Lord Jesus, and shalt believe in thine heart that God hath raised him from the dead, thou shalt be saved.*

INTRODUCTION

Living a Christian life is worth everything considering the finished works of Christ Jesus on the cross. Greatest of all victories a believer has is the victory over death. Abiding in Jesus only, a believer is already above death. This lesson teaches the ways in which we can avoid spiritual and eternal death.

HOW TO AVOID SPIRITUAL AND ETERNAL DEATH

1. **UTILIZE YOUR AUTHORITY OVER DEATH:** (John 17:2, John 10:18) Jesus spoke of power to

die and power rise from death. This power is with us. And we can exercise it by making decision. To avoid eternal death all we need to do is to utilize this power given to us by the death and resurrection of Christ Jesus in speaking forth the confession of eternal life. But this starts from a decision.

2. **RESIST THE FLESH AND LIVE RIGHT:** (Galatians 5:13-17). As the scripture says the flesh profits nothing. Walking or living by the flesh is itself an act of sinking into death. To avoid eternal death believers must strive to continue to live a righteous life. Resisting the flesh will pursue Satan away from you. (James 4:7)

3. **STUDY AND ABIDE IN THE WORD OF GOD:** (John 6: 63; 15: 5).The word of God is a spirit and life itself. It contains all that is necessary to stop one from eternal death. Studying and abiding in it can boost life far away from the possibilities of spiritual death.

SUMMARY

We are overcomers. This means we have conquered the world and everything set as a challenge to us through the world. We not only can avoid spiritual and eternal death but also overpower it if we abide in Jesus for Jesus is in Jesus is life everlasting.

QUESTIONS:

1. Can one avoid spiritual and eternal death?
2. Mention ways in which we can avoid spiritual and eternal death

LESSON 4: HOW TO REACT TO PHYSICAL DEATH AS A BELIEVER

TEXT: Job 2:7 *So went Satan forth from the presence of the LORD, and smote Job with sore boils from the sole of his foot unto his crown.*

MEMORY VERSE: John 11:35 *Jesus wept.*

INTRODUCTION

Reaction to death is one of the most unpredictable actions of people regardless of gender and age, what people can do at the news of death of a beloved person. This lesson is important to all believers because it teaches how all believers should respond or react to death.

HOW TO REACT TO DEATH

1. **CONSIDER THAT LIFE ON EARTH IS TEMPORAL** (Job 7:16-21, Psalm 37:10): As the bible describes it so it is life is short; eternity is endless. As a believer, knowing this prepares your mind towards the breaking news of death.

2. **THE WORLD IS NOT OUR HOME**: (Hebrews 13:14-15) Death is transition: Keep in mind that the world is not our home, and death is a transition, in other words, death is the only means of reaching to our homes. Knowing this

will help to prepare you against the news of death.

3. **WE WILL MEET AGAIN AFTER LIFE** (Luke 16:19-31): Lazarus and the rich man met in the afterlife. This is a reality and not a mere story. Knowing that we will meet again after life, is alone a consolation that we have not lost the dead but rather will be missing them for a while.

4. **THERE IS RESURRECTION:** (John 11:25, 1 Thessalonians 4:16) Jesus rose from the death in order to give us the key of resurrection. Therefore, we will all die and be raised up one day. Knowing this helps us to be ready for death as well as prepares us for any kind of news of death.

5. **OPPORTUNITY TO WORSHIP GOD:** (Job 1:18-22, 2 Samuel 12:21) Believers should learn to return glory to God through worship and praises in the time of sorrow (in all things we are to give thanks to the lord. Doings this, will not only

please God, but also help to absorb the shock which comes with the news of death.

SUMMARY

This is indeed a lesson that every Christian should learn; because over reaction to the news of death is becoming a tradition nowadays that the church even sees nothing wrong in it. Weeping and mourning is not over reaction to death but lost of hope, uncontrollable sadness, multiple ill questionings and calling God names are really an overreaction that shouldn't be heard or seen around Christians. However this can hardly be controlled except the believer works in line with this lesson.

QUESTIONS

1. Is it proper to weep and mourn the death?
2. How should a Christian react to death?

CHAPTER FIVE: RESSURECTION

LESSON 1: RESURRECTION AND ITS TYPES WITH BIBLICAL EXAMPLES

TEXT: 1 Thessalonians 4:16 *For the Lord himself shall descend from heaven with a shout, with the voice of the archangel, and with the trump of God: and the dead in Christ shall rise first: Then we which are alive and remain shall be caught up together with them in the clouds, to meet the Lord in the air: and so shall we ever be with the Lord.*

MEMORY VERSE: John 11:25 *Jesus said unto her, I am the resurrection, and the life: he that believeth in me, though he were dead, yet shall he live:*

INTRODUCTION

Resurrection is one of the biblical and Christian doctrines that is complicated to talk about because of how much it has been argued by unbelievers. Never mind, this is the center of Christian faith; and this is why this lesson is very important. Because it describes the resurrection and revealing its types with biblical examples

What is resurrection?

Resurrection is the coming back to life after death. This could be disbelieved or thought to be a complicated believes as incarnation and re-incarnation among others. Except you believe in Jesus, you can never believe in the concept of resurrection. The bible recorded that the power of God shall raise all who died back to life on the last days and they will wear the same body that was once buried, burnt, lost, or eaten up by wild animals, drowned in the sea, etc as much as the doctrine of resurrection has been an issue of contention, it remains a central believe uphold by many religions of the world.

What are the types of resurrection?

While the main idea of resurrection is still arguable, speaking about its types may simply seem out of context. However, according to biblical knowledge, resurrection can be classified into two types: the resurrection to mortal life and the resurrection to immortal life

1. **THE RESURRECTION FROM MORTAL LIFE**: (John 11:25) Jesus proved Himself the resurrection and life by raising Lazarus (John 11:38-44), Jairus' daughter (Mark 5:21-24), son of the widow from Nain (Luke 7:11-17) and several others unmentioned. This kind of resurrection restores mortal life which in the future will surely die again. Not only Jesus, His disciples (Act 9:39), prophets of the Old Testament (2 Kings 4:8-44) and in our contemporary many

who believed in Jesus have exorcised their faith in this regards.

2. **THE RESURRECTION TO IMMORTAL LIFE**: (John 20:24-29) this is when the dead is raised back to life that cannot die again. This is the resurrection spoken of in the Bible concerning the last days when all who ever died shall rise back to life, wear the same body but different form which can never die again. The only one and perfect example of this kind of resurrection in the Bible is the resurrection of Jesus. After resurrection, Jesus showed himself to His followers, touched them, ate with them and stayed for days before ascending into Heaven with the same body. (Matthew 28:20)

SUMMARY

Resurrection the coming back to life from death needs to be given critical attention by the church and by individual Christians. For in it God reveals His power over sins and death the consequence of sin. God can raise the dead to mortal life as well to immortal

QUESTIONS

1. What is resurrection?
2. What are the types of resurrection?

LESSON 2: THE IMPORTANCE OF THE RESURRECTION TO THE CHURCH

TEXT: 1 Corinthians 15:14 *And if Christ be not risen, then is our preaching vain, and your faith is also vain.*

MEMORY VERSE: Acts 2:24 *Whom God hath raised up, having loosed the pains of death: because it was not possible that he should be holden of it.*

INTRODUCTION:

The Bible if without the resurrection of Jesus would be only a piece of Literature and Christianity confusion. The resurrection of Jesus remains the centre of our Christian faith. This lesson outlines the importance of resurrection to the church of God.

The importances of resurrection to the church are:

1. **RESURRECTION OF JESUS IS EVIDENCE THAT OUR SINS ARE FORGIVEN AND DEATH HAS BEEN CONQUERED:** (1 Corinthians 15:17-18) Of course, even though Jesus died, he would not have been able to defeat death and pay for our sins if it weren't for his resurrection. This explains why it is the case; death was brought to humanity by the sin of mankind through Adam. Since Jesus came to pay

the price for our sin, he has a greater problem to save us from than sin, namely death (Colossians 2:14-15). He only paid for our sin when he died, and after that, he had a lot to fight with death. But because He rose from the dead, He not only delivered us from death, but also defeated it on our behalf. That means we are not currently subject to the bondage that Adam imposed upon us. Halleluiah!

2. **RESURRECTION OF JESUS IS EVIDENCE OF GOD'S OMNIPOTENT POWER**: (2 Samuel 22:33, Job 42:2) to believe in the resurrection is to believe that God, who created the universe and everything in it possesses the power to control everything, including life and death. We Christians believe in the omnipotence of God and the resurrection of Jesus from death is but one evidence we hold on to. For if Jesus had not raised from death, our faith in the power of God ought to be questioned or perhaps we must need

to prove with many explanation why our God who creates life cannot restore life after death.

3. **RESURRECTION OF JESUS IS EVIDENCE OF THE DIVINITY OF JESUS:** All of the things that Jesus is attributed with saying in the Bible as proof of His divinity or equality with God, as we believed in Christianity, were demonstrated by His resurrection from the dead. Jesus used the image of the temple in the book of John 2:17 to declare that he will rise in three days after being destroyed. He asserted that he had the ability to give his life away and then take it back in John 10:18. He explicitly stated in Luke 24:7 that he would be captured, be slain, and then, on the third day, would rise from the dead. He clarified it in John 12:32 when he said that when he is lifted up, he will bring all people to himself. There are several similar claims, but His resurrection proved it all as result, Resurrection is significant to us.

4. **RESURRECTION OF JESUS IS EVIDENCE OF CONTINUITY OF LIFE AFTER DEATH AND THE REASON OF OUR HOPE OF ETERNITY:** (John 11:25-26) by His resurrection, Jesus assures us that we too shall really have life after death. He cleared the way and made a passage from mortality to immortality for us. Therefore fulfilling His words of John 12:32 where He said he shall draw all men to Himself when He is lifted up. We are not afraid of death, we are living in the hope of living again after death and this is what the resurrection has brought for us

5. **RESURRECTION OF JESUS IS EVIDENCE AND POWER OF THE GOSPEL WE PREACH**: 1 Corinthians 15:12-20 the entire message we preach in Christianity whether of love, power, hope, grace, faith etc is centered around the resurrection of Jesus from death. Resurrection therefore meaningful to us because it is our Gospel.

SUMMARY

Christianity does not consider the resurrection to be a teaching because it is the Christianity itself. Every believer should be able to recall that Jesus rose from the grave and like a creed; it should be the dominant belief and have influence over our faith and actions. If Jesus had not risen from the dead, we would not have been delivered from sin and death, we would not have had any hope of living after death, we would not even have received the Gospel, and we would not have believed that Jesus was the Son of God and God is the Almighty.

QUESTIONS

1. Why is the resurrection important to the church?

2. If you had a choice, would you choose to be a Christian if Jesus has not risen?

LESSON 3: CONDITIONS FOR MANIFESTING IN THE POWER OF THE RESURRECTION

TEXT: Ephesians 1:18-20 *Praying always with all prayer and supplication in the Spirit, and watching thereunto with all perseverance and supplication for all saints; And for me, that utterance may be given unto me, that I may open my mouth boldly, to make known the mystery of the gospel, For which I am an ambassador in bonds: that therein I may speak boldly, as I ought to speak.*

MEMORY VERSE: Philippians 3:10 *That I may know him, and the power of his resurrection, and the fellowship of his sufferings, being made conformable unto his death;*

INTRODUCTION

The resurrection of Jesus has ushered us into the place of power. By it we have received the authority to manifest. However it is unfortunate that many Christians do not manifest in this power not because they don't want it but because they do not know how to go about it. Here in this lesson are certain conditions which must be met in order to manifest in this power.

The conditions required for manifesting in the resurrection power are:

1. **IF YOU BELIEVE (**Mark 9:23, 11:22-25, 16:16-17) this is the first condition before manifesting in resurrection power. Jesus Himself on many occasions spoke about as the key to receiving and provoking miracles. Therefore, if you want to be full of this great power first thing first is to believe that you have been given the authority and all power is already in your hands.

2. **IF YOU DECLARE IT:** declaration is one major way of exercising this kind of great power. God

Himself according to Genesis 1:3 during the creation of the universe exercised powers by the use of words from His mouth. In Numbers 14:28 He said to Moses as I hear you say so shall I do. This is to say that Moses' words have the authority it takes to command manifestations. In 1 Samuel 3:19 it was written that the prophet Samuel from his childhood none of his words fell on empty ground. Job 22:23 and Proverbs 18:20-21 confirms that there is power in our spoken declarations. Therefore to manifest in the resurrection power you must condition yourself to declaring your powerful words.

3. **IF YOU ACT IT**: it is not enough to have faith alone; you must declare it daily and also act it. Now this is where there is a problem for most believers. They find it difficult to act on the power within them. Learn how to act on this available power from these examples: the disciples' faith couldn't stop the storm, likewise

the presence of Jesus in the boat but the storm calmed only when Jesus woke from sleep and acted his powers Matthews 8:26. There are several instances where Jesus acted his powers in the Bible. In John 2:7 the wedding at Cana, He performed the first miracle without praying but with a singular instruction asking them to fill the jars with water. He didn't worry about "what if the water did not change to wine" same thing He did in John 6:1-14 when he fed the crowd. He asked them to sit and wait to be served five loaves of bread and two fishes. To manifest in such power, acting on the authority is required. Sometimes this may require patience, calmness, waiting etc (Mark 11:24).

SUMMARY

The requirements for you to manifest in the resurrection power are as follows: you must believe you received it from the moment Jesus rose from the dead, speak and confess it every day without reservation, and act on it. If you can do all three, nothing can stop you from manifesting.

QUESTIONS

1. Is every Christian powerful?
2. What can we do to access the resurrection power?

LESSON 4: FACTS REGARDING THE RESURRECTION OF JESUS

TEXT: 1 Corinthians 15:42-45 *So also is the resurrection of the dead. It is sown in corruption; it is raised in incorruption: It is sown in dishonour; it is raised in glory: it is sown in weakness; it is raised in power: It is sown a natural body; it is raised a spiritual body. There is a natural body, and there is* *a spiritual body. And so it is written, The first man Adam was made a living soul; the last Adam was made a quickening spirit.*

MEMORY VERSE: 1 Corinthians 15:4 *And that he was buried, and that he rose again the third day according to the scriptures:*

INTRODUCTION

This lesson reveals some basic facts surrounding the resurrection of Jesus. Knowing these facts can bring a Christian into understanding all that the resurrection means and brings to us.

1. **JESUS ROSE ON THE THIRD DAY CONFIRMED TO BE EASTER SUNDAY**: (Mark 16:1-2) there may be contradiction if the three days count of Jesus in the grave is compared to as it is today. From Biblical accounts it is noticed that a day is made of two periods; day and night instead of the four periods as we

know of today which are day, afternoon evening and night.

2. **WOMEN WERE FIRST TO EXPERIENCE RESURRECTION:** (Luke 24:1 the women went to anoint Jesus' dead body when they finally discovered that he has risen from death

3. **THE GRAVE WAS EMPTY:** (Luke 12:24) Apostle Peter went into the tomb to confirm the resurrection then he discovered that it was empty

4. **ANGEL ROLLED THE STONE AND SPOKE WITH THE WOMEN:** Matthew 28:2

5. **SOLDIERS GUARDING THE TOMB WERE ASKED TO KICK AGAINST THE RESURRECTION:** Matthew 28:11-15

6. **THE WHITE LINEN FOR HIS BURIAL WAS FOUND WELL ARRANGED** John 20:5

7. **HE APPEARED TO MANY INCLUDING APOSTLE PAUL** John 20:11-29, Acts 9:5

8. **HE HAD A PERFECT BODY:** John 20:27, Luke 24:29-30 He spoke with His disciples, passed the

night with them, ate with them and even asked Thomas to put his hand into His wounds and feel the scars to confirm that it was Him.

9. **HIS RESURRECTION RESTORED THE HOPE OF HIS DISCIPLES:** the disciples were all afraid that they were not closer seen around Jesus when He was on the cross. Peter especially denied Jesus and returned back to his business of fishing pulling other disciples to himself. Never mind, they all got hope by His resurrection. (Luke 24:34)

10. **HIS RESURRECTION CREATED A PATHWAY FOR OUR RESURRECTION THEREFORE WE SHALL BE RAISED FROM DEATH:** because Jesus has risen, we are now assured that we all shall be raised after dead. (1 Thessalonians 4:16)

11. **HIS RESURRECTION BROUGHT POWER TO US:** (Ephesians 1:19) this evidence of our power; the resurrection of Jesus. He overpowered sin

and death and restore mankind to her original place of authority.

12. **MANY PROPHECIES WERE FULFILLED BY THE RESURRECTION:** (Acts 13:33) *God hath fulfilled the same unto us their children, in that he hath raised up Jesus again; as it is also written in the second psalm, Thou art my Son, this day have I begotten thee.*

Luke the writer here quoted Psalm 2:7 as fulfilled by the resurrection. There are many scriptures that have been fulfilled by the resurrection of Jesus.

13. **THE RESURRECTION IS OUR GOSPEL:** (1 Corinthians 15:12-18) this is why it is said that the resurrection is the centre of our Christian faith.

QUESTIONS

1. **Mention the facts you know about the resurrection of Jesus**

2. Did Jesus actually rise from death; how do you know?

www.ingramcontent.com/pod-product-compliance
Lightning Source LLC
Chambersburg PA
CBHW071334140726
47996CB00005B/1977